workbook•for•women

i love you more

Formerly Titled *When Bad Things Happen to Good Marriages*

w o r k b o o k • f o r • w o m e n

i love you more

Six Sessions on How Everyday Problems
Can Strengthen Your Marriage

Drs. Les & Leslie Parrott

ZONDERVAN™

GRAND RAPIDS, MICHIGAN 49530 USA

ZONDERVAN™

I Love You More Workbook for Women
Copyright © 2001, 2005 by Les and Leslie Parrott
Formerly titled *When Bad Things Happen to Good Marriages Workbook for Women*

Requests for information should be addressed to:

Zondervan, *Grand Rapids, Michigan 49530*

ISBN-10: 0-310-26276-3
ISBN-13: 978-0-310-26276-3

Published in association with Yates & Yates, LLP, Attorneys and Counselors, Suite 1000, Literary Agent, Orange, CA.

Interior design by Beth Shagene

Printed in the United States of America

11 12 /❖ DCI/ 15 14 13 12 11 10 9 8 7 6

contents

A Letter to Our Readers   7

1. Taking Inventory of Your Marriage   9

2. Exploring Your Marital Armament   12

3. Why Every Marriage Has Everyday Problems   14

4. What Did You Expect?   16

5. The Big Question   18

6. So Many Choices   20

7. Your Attitude Quotient   22

8. What Have You Been Looking For?   24

9. Coping with the Invasion of Intimacy   27

10. When Husband and Wife Become Mom and Dad   30

11. Refueling the Sexual Fire   32

12. Taking Control of Your Time-Starved Marriage   35

13. Getting to Know You . . . All over Again   37

14. Healing Your Painful Past   40

15. Owning Up   42

16. High Hopes—Even When You're Hurting   45

17. Walking in Your Partner's Shoes   48

18. Assessing Your Spiritual Language   50

19. Finding the Inspiration around You   52

20. Taking Cover from a Bombshell and Its Fallout   55

21. Surviving Your Private Gethsemane   57

Small Group Discussion Guide   59

a letter to our readers

"I took a speed reading course and read *War and Peace* in twenty minutes," says comedian Woody Allen. "It involves Russia."

Ever felt like that after reading a book? Sometimes it becomes so easy to focus on finishing a book that we miss its main message. What you hold in your hand is a kind of insurance policy against that happening while you are reading *I Love You More*. But it's more than that too.

Books let us shake hands with new ideas. But these ideas remain as flat as the printed page if we do not apply them to our lives. For this reason, we have designed workbooks—one for husbands and one for wives—that will help you incorporate into your marriage the new lessons you learn while reading.

As you read through the main book, you will discover places where it points you to do an exercise in these workbooks. Most of them are designed for you to take about five minutes on your own to complete a few questions or to take a brief self-test and then compare your results with your spouse (that's why it's important for each spouse to have a workbook). Or, it may give you an exercise to do together so that you can put into practice a new principle. This is where real learning occurs. This is where new ideas become more than acquaintances; they begin to make a positive difference in your marriage.

We have used these exercises with countless couples, both in our counseling practice as well as in our seminar settings. They are proven. They work. And that's why we are passionate about you doing them as you read through our book.

While there is no one right way to use these workbooks, we suggest that you complete the exercises as you encounter them in the book, or soon after you have finished reading the chapter that covers the exercise. In other words, try to complete the exercises for that chapter before moving on to the next one. The point is to integrate the exercises into the process of reading the book. Some of the exercises are designed to be used again and again ("The Big Question," for example), helping you continue to deepen your level of intimacy. Others are more of a one-shot exercise designed to give you a flash of insight.

As you proceed through the pages of this book, make it your own. Don't get too hung up on following the rules. If a particular exercise leads you down a more intriguing path, take it. Some of these exercises may simply serve as springboards to discussions that fit your style more appropriately. However, if an exercise seems a bit challenging, don't give up on it. As the saying goes, anything worth having is worth working for—especially when it comes to marriage.

So, whether you are a speed reader or not, we hope you don't approach *I Love You More* just to check it off your "to-do" list. We hope and pray that you will, instead, use these exercises, self-tests, and discussion questions to internalize the book's message and fortify your marriage with every possible good thing.

LES AND LESLIE PARROTT

taking inventory
of your marriage

Every couple bumps into bad things—circumstances that make marriage more difficult. In this first exercise, we urge you to take an inventory of everything threatening your love. Every couple has their own unique list. What follows are some of the most common. Take a moment, without input from your spouse, to check those that currently top your list.

- ☐ Frequent conflict
- ☐ Financial pressures
- ☐ Power struggles
- ☐ Busy schedules
- ☐ Work pressures
- ☐ Career crisis
- ☐ Infertility
- ☐ Tumultuous relations with extended family
- ☐ A rebellious child
- ☐ Sexual unfulfillment
- ☐ Lack of spiritual intimacy
- ☐ Frequent communication breakdowns
- ☐ Major illness
- ☐ Addictions

- ☐ Infidelities and lack of trust
- ☐ Grief or loss
- ☐ Other: _____

Before discussing the list you just made with your partner, take a few more minutes to note the things in your life right now that are good for your marriage. What half-dozen good things are augmenting the love you share? Your list could consist of anything from "having a date night each week" to "being honest with each other" to "sharing the housework." Note what is currently going on that buoys your marriage in spite of everything else.

- ☐ Being honest with each other
- ☐ Sharing housework
- ☐ Sharing humor or laughter
- ☐ Having strong social support
- ☐ Sharing a vision for our future
- ☐ Enjoying a committed church life together
- ☐ Enjoying a fulfilling sex life
- ☐ Having a date night
- ☐ Enjoying good children
- ☐ Feeling in good physical health
- ☐ Having a secure financial future
- ☐ Sharing interests and hobbies
- ☐ Enjoying strong extended family relationships
- ☐ Supporting each other in prayer
- ☐ Feeling secure in our marriage commitment
- ☐ Feeling strong emotional health
- ☐ Other: _____

Once you've made your two lists, set aside some time to share this information with each other. Don't turn this into a gripe session. The point of sharing your first list is to simply identify what difficult things you are both contending with that impact your marriage. The goal in sharing your second list is to remember the positive, not just the negative.

exploring your marital armament

This brief exercise requires honesty, sensitivity, and self-reflection. As you read in the book, research has revealed five qualities that are the armament used to protect couples from the destruction of bad things:

1. Ownership	taking responsibility for what you do and say
2. Hope	believing that good is a part of your future
3. Empathy	putting yourself in your partner's shoes
4. Forgiveness	letting go of resentment and making things right
5. Commitment	doing all you can to make your relationship rock solid

As you consider these qualities, rate where you, and then your partner, are on each one. Do this on your own, without consulting your husband for now.

You as a Wife						
Shift Blame	1	2	3	4	5	Take Ownership
Pessimistic	1	2	3	4	5	Optimistic
Self-Consumed	1	2	3	4	5	Empathic
Resentful	1	2	3	4	5	Forgiving
Give Up Easily	1	2	3	4	5	Fully Committed

Your Husband						
Shift Blame	1	2	3	4	5	Take Ownership
Pessimistic	1	2	3	4	5	Optimistic
Self-Consumed	1	2	3	4	5	Empathic
Resentful	1	2	3	4	5	Forgiving
Give Up Easily	1	2	3	4	5	Fully Committed

After both you and your partner have rated these qualities on your own, take a few minutes to discuss your results. It is important to stay objective in this discussion. Focus on being sensitive to your partner's feelings and being open to what your partner has to say. The goal is to learn what both of you bring to your joint efforts in battling the negative things.

why every marriage has everyday problems

The more you understand *why* problems happen in good marriages, the better equipped you are to transcend them. Knowing *why* empowers our *how*. So this simple exercise is devoted to helping you, on your own without your partner's input for now, identify which causal factors are most likely to sabotage your relationship. Begin by reflecting for a moment on some of the difficulties your marriage has faced. If you were to sum up your explanation for *why* these things have happened, how would you put it?

Next, review the list of explanations given in the book and rank them from 1 (the most accurate reason that applies to your marriage) to 5 (the least accurate reason your marriage has bumped into bad things).

The main reason for our marriage experiencing difficulty right now is . . .

☐ My Idealistic Expectations
☐ My Restless Sense of Self
☐ My Lack of Relationship Skills
☐ My Unhealthy Choices
☐ Our Unfortunate Circumstances

Once you have given each of these potential reasons a ranking, share them with your partner and compare your answers as you discuss why your good marriage is most vulnerable to bad things.

what did you expect?

Most unrealistic expectations we have about our marriage are fueled by thoughts and feelings we are not even aware of. For example, we may have an expectation about how our partner is to care for the yard or prepare a meal—something we've never really articulated to ourselves or anyone else—but only when our partner doesn't fulfill our expectation do we become aware of how important our expectation is. As you look back over your married life, what unrealistic expectations can you identify?

To help you identify more specific expectations that are not getting met in your marriage, consider the following list of common expectations and note which ones you used to have and which ones you still are holding on to today:

	In the Past	Still Expecting	New Expectation
My spouse should . . .			
Always listen attentively	_____	_____	_____
Stay at home with the kids	_____	_____	_____
Work full-time	_____	_____	_____
Manage the family finances	_____	_____	_____
Do the yard work	_____	_____	_____
Care for our automobile(s)	_____	_____	_____
Prepare a hot meal each evening	_____	_____	_____
Schedule social events	_____	_____	_____
Do the grocery shopping	_____	_____	_____
Surprise me with gifts on occasion	_____	_____	_____
Plan our vacations	_____	_____	_____
Initiate sex	_____	_____	_____
Keep the house clean	_____	_____	_____
Want to discuss our relationship	_____	_____	_____
Know what I'm thinking	_____	_____	_____
Go to bed when I do	_____	_____	_____
Consult me on decisions	_____	_____	_____
Discipline our children	_____	_____	_____
Plan our date nights	_____	_____	_____
Other:_____	_____	_____	_____

Once you have noted your expectations, both from the past and the present, share your lists with each other and keep in mind that this is simply an exercise in sharing information. We will get to solutions to unrealistic expectations shortly.

the big question

You've read about how we all have blind spots that only our spouse can help us see. This exercise will facilitate a healthy exchange between the two of you so that you can discuss these with a minimum of defensiveness. This is an exercise, by the way, that you can do on a weekly or monthly basis. It takes no more than ten minutes, and here's how it works.

1. Ask your husband if he is willing, along with you, to answer "The Big Question": What would make me a better spouse?

2. If he agrees, prepare your mind to be objective and open to giving as well as receiving personal information. Lower your guard and warm your heart.

3. On scratch paper, note one thing your husband could do right now to be a better marriage partner to you.

4. On that same paper, note one thing that already makes your husband a good marriage partner to you right now. Be sure you have in mind an example from the past week that backs up your point and makes it concrete.

5. Once you have both made your notes of one good thing and one area for improvement, take turns sharing what you have.

6. Finally, don't nag your husband about how he could improve—make your suggestion during this exercise and then leave it there, until the next time you do The Big Question.

so many choices

Geoffrey Fisher, former archbishop of Canterbury, once noted that every man and woman makes personal choices in the "sacred realm of privacy." At the risk of being too bold, we ask you, in this exercise, to allow your spouse into this sacred realm and explore the choices you both have made—choices that have served as a rudder to your marriage. These are choices that have brought your marriage to the place it is today. The book notes several examples of negative kinds of choices (keeping information private, withholding sex, going into debt, breaking a confidence with your spouse, not seeking counseling when you needed it, etc.). Take a moment right now to note a half-dozen personal choices that are relevant; three choices for the better and three for the worse.

Three choices I/we made that improved our marriage:

1.

2.

3.

Three choices I/we made that worsened our marriage:

1.

2.

3.

As you review these choices, what can you learn to improve your decision making as it relates to your relationship?

your attitude quotient

You are engaging in self-talk every minute of your waking life. You use this internal thought language to interpret the world. And it is your self-talk that forms the basis for your attitude. This quick exercise will help you assess your attitude. Simply rate how much you agree with each of these statements by using the following scale.

1	Strongly disagree
2	Disagree
3	Not sure
4	Agree
5	Strongly agree

	1	2	3	4	5
I believe the maxim that says, "A zebra cannot change his stripes."	1	2	3	4	5
If there is something wrong, I'll notice it.	1	2	3	4	5
It is almost impossible to overcome the influences of the past.	1	2	3	4	5
Sometimes the littlest thing can ruin my day.	1	2	3	4	5
I tend to be more grumpy when the weather's bad.	1	2	3	4	5
Some difficulties cannot be made better.	1	2	3	4	5
If something doesn't work, I tend to give up.	1	2	3	4	5
Nothing in life is free.	1	2	3	4	5
I rarely get my share of the pie.	1	2	3	4	5
There's always someone to blame.	1	2	3	4	5

Total "NT" Score _____

Once you have added up your ratings for this list—what we call your "NT" score—proceed to the next list of statements and do the same thing.

If a person wants to, he can be happy under almost any circumstances.	1	2	3	4	5
I like the respect of others, but if I don't get it I'm not going to stew about it.	1	2	3	4	5
People are disturbed not by situations but by the view they take of them.	1	2	3	4	5
I cause my own moods.	1	2	3	4	5
I believe that something good is around the corner.					
Just because something once affected your life doesn't mean it needs to still do so.	1	2	3	4	5
People are basically trustworthy.	1	2	3	4	5
I'm optimistic about the future.	1	2	3	4	5
I'm good at adjusting to things beyond my control.	1	2	3	4	5
People describe me as having a thick skin.	1	2	3	4	5

Total "PT" Score _____

Add up your ratings for this list. It is your "PT" score.

Your NT score indicates the degree of negative thinking you tend to engage in. Your PT score indicates the degree of positive thinking you tend to do. By comparing these numbers, you can begin to determine whether you do more positive thinking than negative, or the other way around. If you both feel comfortable doing so, compare your scores with your spouse's scores.

what have you been looking for?

Everyone is looking for something—especially in marriage. We call it your mind-set, and understanding your marriage mind-set is one of the most important exercises a spouse can do. Your mind-set, after all, has nothing to do with anyone but you. This exercise will help you become aware of what you are looking for in your spouse and whether it is helpful to your marriage.

We all view our partner through a series of filters. Below is a list of these filters. Look through this list of filters and check the six or so that are most descriptive of the ways you view your partner.

☐ Accepting	☐ Cold	☐ Friendly
☐ Adaptable	☐ Confident	☐ Gentle
☐ Aggressive	☐ Conforming	☐ Giving
☐ Annoying	☐ Controlling	☐ Greedy
☐ Anxious	☐ Critical	☐ Gruff
☐ Bitter	☐ Demanding	☐ Gullible
☐ Brave	☐ Dependable	☐ Helpful
☐ Calm	☐ Dependent	☐ Helpless
☐ Carefree	☐ Determined	☐ Idealistic
☐ Careless	☐ Disciplined	☐ Inconsiderate
☐ Caring	☐ Efficient	☐ Innovative
☐ Cheerful	☐ Elusive	☐ Insensitive
☐ Clever	☐ Energetic	☐ Intelligent

☐ Irresponsible	☐ Perfectionist	☐ Self-conscious
☐ Irritable	☐ Petty	☐ Self-righteous
☐ Jealous	☐ Playful	☐ Spontaneous
☐ Kind	☐ Principled	☐ Stubborn
☐ Lazy	☐ Protective	☐ Tactful
☐ Manipulative	☐ Rational	☐ Tender
☐ Naïve	☐ Reactionary	☐ Trusting
☐ Narcissistic	☐ Reasonable	☐ Trustworthy
☐ Negative	☐ Reassuring	☐ Understanding
☐ Noisy	☐ Regretful	☐ Unpredictable
☐ Objective	☐ Relaxed	☐ Visionary
☐ Oblivious	☐ Reliable	☐ Witty
☐ Passive	☐ Respectful	☐ Worried
☐ Patient	☐ Rigid	

Once you have checked the top half-dozen ways you tend to view your spouse, determine whether they are mostly positive or mostly negative. The list is composed of forty filters in each category. In the space below, note the negative filters you tend to view your spouse through and when you are most likely to use them.

Filter: _____ I see this quality when my spouse _____

_____.

Filter: _____ I see this quality when my spouse _____

_____.

Filter: _____ I see this quality when my spouse _____

_____.

Filter: _____ I see this quality when my spouse _____
_____.

Filter:_____ I see this quality when my spouse _____
_____.

Filter:_____ I see this quality when my spouse _____
_____.

Filter: _____ I see this quality when my spouse _____
_____.

Next, consider ways that you might counter your negative filters with a more positive mind-set. You might ask your partner
for ways that you could view a situation or a specific behavior
more positively. You may want to consider the four steps outlined in chapter 4 and see how they might apply to your potentially negative mind-set. With an open mind, this discussion can
be a turning point in changing your mind-set, not to mention
your marriage, for the better.

coping with the invasion of intimacy

Not every spouse sees this issue as a significant one. So before going much further, rate how intimacy has become an invasion for you in your marriage on the following scale.

Not a problem									Major problem
1	2	3	4	5	6	7	8	9	10

Now rate on this same scale how you think your spouse might answer. Next, compare how your husband answered with how you thought he would.

If either you or your spouse rated this issue at a five or higher, continue on with this exercise to more effectively put into practice coping strategies for your situation.

The book suggests that you make known to your spouse what is off limits for you because it is too vulnerable, too painful. In specific terms, what topics of conversation, what incidents, what secrets do you need to underscore with your spouse? Briefly note these tender spots and explain to your partner why these things are off limits.

The book also suggests that you create personal space by drawing some boundary lines. For example, if you need time to decompress at the end of the day before you jump into a conversation or before you get hit with a list of errands or things you need to do, make your needs explicitly known. Maybe you need an evening a month with your friends to maintain that connection. Whatever it is, in the space below note specific things that would help you gain the space you need to become more fully present with your husband, and then share it with him.

The book suggests one more thing that will help you cope with an overabundance of intimacy: Draw a property line. What personal items do you want left alone? Perhaps it is your newspaper, a special pen you keep on your desk, or any number of things that you are especially wanting to be sure are left the way you want them. Make these known in the space below and share them with your spouse.

when husband and wife become mom and dad

As the book points out, a new mom and a new dad each have their own role in keeping a good marriage going. Dads need to work at entering their wives' new world, and moms need to give their husbands space to do so. For this reason, the exercises for this section in your two workbooks are quite different but will take you toward the same goal.

Especially for moms: As you read in the book, the majority of wives experience a huge plummet in their marital satisfaction in the year after their first baby arrives. This dissatisfaction can continue for years if you do not make changes in your marriage. This is especially true for wives who are holding onto an ideal of romance that becomes somewhat impractical as you enter parenthood. As we said in the book, the more stock you put in romance before the baby was born, the more loss you will feel when your busy husband seems disconnected. So take a moment right now to consider your view of romance.

I define romance as _____

I know my husband is becoming less romantic when . . .

This change in our level of romance is due to his becoming a father . . .

- ☐ 5 percent of the time or less
- ☐ 50 percent of the time or less
- ☐ Almost all the time

If you see your change in romance as due to your husband becoming a father, what can you do to acknowledge his new role and adjust your expectations of romance, at least for a while? In other words, what smaller acts of romance can you now learn to cherish as you are becoming parents together?

If you see your change in romance as not due to your husband's new role as a father, discuss with him why you think this is happening and brainstorm solutions together.

refueling the sexual fire

Talking about sex with your spouse can be an intimidating experience. You may have had previous discussions in this area that only made matters worse. In this exercise, we want to guide you in a healthy, productive discussion with one primary goal: to understand each other's sexuality better. So set aside preconceived notions and focus on understanding—first, yourself, and then your spouse's sexuality.

Begin by rating your sexual desire in general on the following scale:

Weak sexual desire   **Strong sexual desire**

1	2	3	4	5	6	7	8	9	10

Next, consider how many times in a month you would ideally like to have sex with your spouse.

☐ Less than once a month
☐ Once a month
☐ Twice a month
☐ Once a week
☐ Twice a week or more

How do you know when your partner would like to have sex? What signs do you watch for?

How do you like sex to be initiated in your relationship? Is this something you like to do, or do you prefer your partner do this, and if so, how?

In your opinion, what is the major roadblock to enjoying sex with your partner? Is it busy schedules, lack of desire, hygiene, interruptions, shortage of romance? Identify what makes it difficult for you, personally, to enjoy a fulfilling sex life. If you do not have anything that is an impediment from your perspective, identify what you think your spouse might say.

Once you have completed these questions, take time to discuss your answers with each other. Are your levels of sexual desire quite different? If so, are you able to understand and make adjustments to your partner's level of desire? To do this, begin by identifying times when the two of you are most in synch sexually.

We are most sexually in synch when (we have had a date night, we have prayed together, we are away from the kids, we have both had a shower, etc.) . . .

Keep in mind that the goal of your conversation is simply to understand your partner's sexuality and think constructively about how you can create a more fulfilling sex life together. With this in mind, we urge you to brainstorm more things you can do as a couple to improve your sex life.

taking control
of your time-starved marriage

Since you are motivated to read our book and do these workbook exercises, we know that your marriage is a high priority for you. In this exercise, however, we want you to get more clear than you have ever been about this priority. More important, we want what you *say* about your marriage being important to match what you *do* about it.

You can begin to gain control of your time-starved marriage by taking a moment to answer a few basic questions.

How much time do you spend together in a typical workday? _____

How much time do you spend together in a typical weekend? _____

Total number of hours you spend together in an average week: _____

How do you spend the waking hours you have together each week? List as many specific activities as you can recall from a typical week.

Review the list you just made and circle the three most important activities you do together. Would you like more time to do these? If so, identify specific things you can do to create more time for them (e.g., eliminate another activity, start a baby-sitting co-op, schedule it in our calendars). The more specific you are, the better.

What things were not on your list but you wish they were? In other words, what do you wish you did together as a couple, but never seem to find the time for?

The key for most busy couples is making time for those activities that are not urgent but are important. The things you would like to have more time for get swallowed by urgent things that sometimes matter and sometimes don't. If you want to have a date night once a week, for example, you will need to protect that time ferociously. Take time now to discuss with your spouse ways you will make your non-urgent, but important activities in your marriage a top priority by giving them the time they deserve.

getting to know you . . . all over again

This is an exercise designed to help you set the wheels in motion for reconnecting with your spouse. We begin with a brief assessment of simple questions:

Y	N	Has your sexual interest in each other waned in the last few months or years?
Y	N	Do you find yourself looking for alternatives to being with your spouse?
Y	N	Has celebrating his birthday become just another thing on your "to do" list?
Y	N	Do you depend less and less on your partner for information and activity?
Y	N	Do you deliberately plan events apart from your spouse?
Y	N	Have you quit sharing the details of your life with your spouse?
Y	N	If you have a choice, would you prefer to be with friends rather than your spouse?

The more you answered "Yes" to these questions, the wider the gap between you and your spouse. The question, of course, is how to bring the two of you closer together. And the key is getting reacquainted. Literally. Consider the following questions regarding your spouse:

1. What is his favorite recent movie?

2. What has he learned about himself in the past year?

3. What worries him the most right now?

4. What has he recently been thinking about his parents?

5. What is he most proud of doing in the last month?

6. What does he like most about you right now?

7. What is his favorite childhood memory?

8. What has touched him most deeply in recent days?

9. What is the best part of his day?

Can you answer these questions? This is just a start, but these kinds of questions will help you get to know your partner and bring you closer together. Take some time to explore these and other issues with him.

There are a couple more things we suggest in this exercise. Identify for yourself what is taking precedence over your marriage. Is your work, your activities at church, your children, your addiction, your painful past, or anything else crowding you out of time with your spouse? Take a serious look at your life right now, and if you see that something is keeping you from your marriage, write it down. Labeling it is the first step in changing it. So write it down and take a stab at identifying how you can keep it from further crowding out your marriage.

Next, make note of a specific plan to get away for a weekend together. In the space below, write down where, when, and how you might get away together within the next four weeks. Then look over the list of questions from the beginning of this exercise and add to it. What can you ask your spouse in order to get reacquainted with him? Make your list of questions here:

As the two of you steal away for your weekend together, make getting to know him your top goal. Explore the list of questions together, and reconnect with parts of your partner you have too long neglected.

healing your painful past

This is not an exercise for everyone. Because we all have unique, personal stories, some will find this more helpful than others. It is designed to be a tool for talking to your partner about the pain from your past as a way to begin its healing.

Reflect on your personal history and make note of any memories you have of feeling hurt. The point here is not to dredge up minor offenses you have suffered, but rather more significant betrayals or injustices you have endured. No need to record all the details, just make a note of what it is that comes to mind.

As you explore these painful memories in your own mind, consider how they may have or are still impacting the way you relate to your spouse. This is your "unfinished business." If you feel safe enough, invite your spouse into this process by asking him to hear your story. Then, see if he has any ideas or theories about how your painful past continues to impact your present marriage. If you would like, you can record the insights you both might have in the following space.

As we note in the book, we urge you to seek help from a professional counselor if you believe previous pain is causing you marital difficulties. There are simply too many personal variables for you to make much long-term progress from a brief exercise. And be assured that there is hope for overcoming your painful past. In time, you will discover that this healing process has given you an unspeakable depth of connection to your partner and brought you to a marriage you've only dreamed about.

owning up

Taking responsibility for the state of your marriage can be one of the most challenging and humiliating actions a spouse ever faces. It is far easier to point fingers and lay blame than it is to stand up and say, "The buck stops here." This exercise, however, is designed to help you do just that.

How would you rate the current state of your marriage?

Lousy									Outstanding
1	2	3	4	5	6	7	8	9	10

How do you think your partner would rate the current state of your marriage?

Lousy									Outstanding
1	2	3	4	5	6	7	8	9	10

How much are you responsible for its current condition?

No responsibility									Complete responsibility
1	2	3	4	5	6	7	8	9	10

How much responsibility do you think your partner would take for the current state of your marriage?

No responsibility									Complete responsibility
1	2	3	4	5	6	7	8	9	10

At this point, if you feel safe enough, share and discuss the results of this part of the exercise with each other. Compare your answers and explain to each other why you answered the way you did.

Next, do your best to set aside your impulse to shift blame for anything that is not the way you want it in your marriage and identify in specific terms what you (though it may not be you alone) are responsible for. Don't get caught up in why you are not solely responsible; let that go for now and simply identify what you bring to the current state of your marriage.

I am responsible for _____

I am responsible for _____

I am responsible for _____

Share these things with your spouse. As you listen to him talk about what he is responsible for, do not compound his guilt. Simply listen carefully and be sure that he knows you are listening with a compassionate ear. You may want to take this exercise a step further—now or later—and identify what you will do about the things you know you are responsible for. You can use this space to identify one thing you will start or stop doing because you are responsible.

By the way, this is where accountability really pays off. Consider the idea of talking to a trusted friend who will keep your feet to the fire, a friend who will ask you routinely how you are doing at changing the behavior you have targeted.

high hopes—
even when you're hurting

Once you have established a reasonable level of responsibility, hope begins to bloom. You can't expect it to be soaring, but in time it will grow. For now, it is important to honestly determine how much you have. If your marriage ran on a tank of hope, where would the needle that measures its level be? Are you recently refueled, or are you running on fumes? Draw in the needle on this "hope gauge."

Many experts believe that optimism and hope are contagious. If your hope is sagging, consider someone, perhaps another couple you know, who has high hopes. Study them. What is it about their personality, their character, that cultivates hope? And if you think it's just "luck," think again. Optimistic people aren't lucky at all. They have disciplined themselves to see the light at the end of the tunnel when others think there is no end to their troubles in sight. Once you have identified a good model of hope, list two or three qualities that you think contribute to their optimism.

1.

2.

3.

What can you learn from them? Would you ever consider asking this person or this couple to be your hope mentors? Remember that if your marriage is to successfully battle bad things, you will need an ample supply of hope. So you must do all you can to cultivate it—even be mentored in it.

The bottom line is that hope has to do with the picture you have of your future. Take a moment right now to carefully envision the future of your marriage. What does it look like a year from now? Paint your picture with as many details as possible by completing these sentences:

The thing that worries me most about our future is . . .

The thing that gives me the most hope for the future of our marriage is . . .

A year from now, we will . . .

In time, our marriage will be better than it is today because . . .

Share your answers with one another and discuss your future together by identifying the dreams and hopes you hold about it.

walking in your partner's shoes

In the book, we point out that to really practice empathy, you must use both your heart and your head. In other words, empathy requires both a feeling and a thinking component. Like two wings of an airplane, empathy needs your capacity to sympathize as well as analyze. And if you are like most people, you are probably better at loving more with either your head or your heart. Take this quick test to uncover your love style.

1. When my husband brings home a problem, I usually try to . . .
   a. solve it so he is less troubled.
   b. simply let him know I understand.

2. If my husband has a cold or allergy and needs something from the pharmacy, I typically . . .
   a. try to get it when I am out on other errands.
   b. drop everything else to get it as soon as possible.

3. When my husband is experiencing deep emotions, I try to . . .
   a. help him get them under control.
   b. feel the same feelings with him.

4. Which describes you better?
   a. I tend to be objective.
   b. I tend to be sympathetic.

The more times you answered with "a," the more likely you are to love with your head. The more times you answered with "b," the more likely you are to love with your heart. This is clearly not a definitive test, just a tool to get you reflecting on your style. More often than not, the husband is more analytical and the wife is more sympathetic, but not always. The point is that empathy requires both the capacity to feel with another person and the objective capacity to step back and see how accurately those feelings match our partner's. Take another stab at assessing where you are by marking the following scale:

Thinking									Feeling
1	2	3	4	5	6	7	8	9	10

To improve your empathy skills, think of a specific recent situation that involved a misunderstanding—big or small—with your spouse. As you recount this experience, try to see it from his point of view. Why do you think he may have reacted or felt the way he did at that moment? Make a quick note of what you think was going on for him.

Now, ask your husband to rate how accurate your perceptions are on a scale of 1 to 10. Do this simple exercise as many times as you can in the next week or so. The more you do it, the more accurate you will become, and the more empathy you will have for each other.

49

assessing your spiritual language

Understanding what spiritual language you tend to speak most often can be enlightening, to say the very least, for most of us. And when you understand the spiritual language your spouse speaks, it can be revolutionary. After reviewing the nine differing pathways to God that are outlined in the book, rank the top two or three styles that fit you, and then your spouse, best.

Me	My husband	The Pathway of . . .
_____	_____	*Tradition*: loving God through rituals, sacraments, and symbols.
_____	_____	*Vision*: loving God by dreaming a great dream.
_____	_____	*Relationships*: loving God by being around other people.
_____	_____	*Intellectual Thought*: seeking God with the mind.
_____	_____	*Service*: loving God by loving others.
_____	_____	*Contemplation*: loving God in a quiet pursuit.
_____	_____	*Activism*: loving God by warring against injustice.
_____	_____	*Nature*: feeling closest to God in the outdoors.
_____	_____	*Worship*: loving God through joyful celebration.

Now jot down some specific ways these are manifested in your life. If you are a contemplative, for example, what do you like to do, where do you like to go, how much time do you like to spend, to be close to God?

Once you and your spouse have both noted the top two or three styles that fit you best, spend a few minutes comparing them. Discuss what you might learn from each other's pathways if they are different.

finding the inspiration around you

The cultivation of inspiration is one of the most defining qualities of couples who have learned to become soul mates. As you walk together with God, few things will join your spirits like a moment that inspires both of you. This exercise will help you recount these moments and find new ones.

What happens within you, personally, when you are inspired by something you've read, heard, or seen? Do you have a physiological response? Are you more motivated? What about your emotions? Consider these questions and begin this exercise by completing this sentence: *I know I've been inspired when . . .*

Next, note the last time you were truly inspired (How long ago was it? What inspired you? Did you share it with anyone?):

Note two or three of the most inspirational moments of your entire life and why they stand out to you (consider speeches or sermons you've heard, books you've read, movies you've seen, people you've met, and so on):

Now consider how you can bring more inspirational moments into your marriage by answering the following questions together as a couple:

1. What kinds of places are we most likely to encounter inspirational moments (e.g., a site with historical significance, our church, hiking in the wilderness)?

2. Where are we as a couple likely to encounter people who might inspire us (e.g., a volunteer agency, a children's center)?

3. What things can we do together that would heighten our inspiration quotient (e.g., rent movies of motivational stories, read a biography of a couple who overcame something that seemed insurmountable)?

4. What couples can we socialize with or even ask to mentor us who would likely bring more inspirational moments into our marriage (e.g., an older couple at church who has a story to tell)?

Inspirational moments cannot be coerced or conjured up at will. They are discovered. Spontaneously. But we can avail our spirits of the places, the people, and the experiences where they are more likely to occur. As you review your answers to the previous questions together, make a commitment to look for the inspiration around you. As you've learned from the book, if we keep our eyes open, we often find what we are looking for.

taking cover from a bombshell and its fallout

The goal of this exercise is to help you ease into the appendix by giving you and your partner an opportunity to explore whatever crisis has struck your relationship. Take some time to explore the following issues, and you will be better equipped to move forward to some of the specific issues in this chapter.

To begin with, consider what you expected from married life. An earlier exercise in this workbook helped you explore some potentially unrealistic expectations most of us carry into this relationship, but what we are asking about here is your big picture. Talk to your partner about that picture. Did you ever imagine facing a crisis together? If so, what did you envision?

Next, explore how your particular marriage crisis shook you personally. Describe in specific terms how it has impacted you.

Complete the following sentences to help you clarify the impact of your crisis.

Before our marriage crisis _____

After our marriage crisis _____

The worst thing for my spouse involving our crisis _____

The best thing for my spouse involving our crisis _____

The worst thing for me to come out of our crisis _____

The best thing for me to come out of our crisis _____

If you feel safe enough, share with each other what you have gained from completing this exercise.

surviving your private gethsemane

Every couple who is jolted by a personal crisis—a private Gethsemane—is left wondering what to do to survive it. In this exercise we give you some concrete steps to consider.

First, acknowledge the loss. Things are not the same since your jolt. What have you lost? Make a list of everything that comes to mind, not just the obvious. For example, if your spouse has become a gambling addict, you have not only lost money because of the addiction, you have lost the spontaneity to go places where he may be especially tempted to gamble. You have lost the freedom to watch certain television programs because of it, and so on. Make a list of your losses.

Being aware of what you have lost is crucial to recovery. It will help you transcend denial and become more clearheaded and healthy. Next, assess where you are on your road to coming back from this jolt. Be honest and use the following scale if it is helpful.

In hopeless despair								Hopeful and moving on
1	2	3	4	5	6	7	8	9	10

If you are rating your situation as more hopeless than hopeful, what can you do, in specific terms (e.g., start a support group), that you are not already doing to make your recovery from this jolt more complete?

How will your marriage be stronger as a result of battling this crisis and overcoming this jolt?

If you feel safe enough, discuss this exercise with your partner.

for small group discussion with the dvd curriculum

Studying this material in a small group with other couples is one of the best ways to make it stick—and have a lot of fun in the process.

In the following pages you will find discussion questions you can use in each of your six small group sessions. Don't get hung up on answering every one of them in order. Use the questions that work best for the personality of your group.

You will see that some of the sessions are based on more than one chapter from the book. You'll also discover that not all chapters in the book are covered in these sessions. Why? Because most groups feel that six sessions is just about the right length for a small group series. Of course, you can feel free to bring into your group discussions the content you'd like to explore for the chapters that are not highlighted in your six sessions.

Obviously, you are going to get more out of the discussion if you've read the pertinent chapters. But if you haven't read them, don't worry. You can still join in on the discussion and you don't need to feel an ounce of guilt. The purpose is to enjoy the interaction and learn from it. You can read the chapters later on if you wish.

You'll also find that each of the sessions will rely on an exercise or two from this workbook. We've selected exercises that will not put anyone on the spot or force anyone to share information they don't want to. Of course, your group may elect to use other exercises from this workbook to discuss if you wish. That's up to you and your group.

A key ingredient to successful small group discussion is vulnerability. Typically, the more transparent you are, the more meaningful the experience will be. And the more open others will be as well. Vulnerability begets vulnerability. However, we caution you not to use this time to gripe about your partner in some way. Don't embarrass each other by dragging out dirty laundry you know would upset your partner. Of course, this can cause each of you to walk a narrow line. You want to be genuine and vulnerable, but not at the expense of your partner's feelings.

Another key ingredient in these discussions is specificity. You'll gain much more out of this time when you use specific examples with each other. So with this in mind, we will remind you to "be specific" every so often.

If you have the time, there is also a section at the end of each session that gives the two of you something to do in the days following your group time together. These exercises are found in this workbook and will help you discover more ways you can encourage each other and internalize the content of *I Love You More*.

One more thing. Each session begins with a question that is "just for fun"—a kind of icebreaker. We've selected one question from our book *Love Talk Starters* which contains more than three hundred similar kinds of questions. They are just to get the wheels turning as you come together as a group. You can order this little book of fun questions at www.RealRelationships.com.

So relax. Have fun. And learn all you can to love each other more.

SESSION ONE

love is not enough

A marriage survives and thrives when a couple learns
to use problems to their advantage.
(Based on chapters 1 and 2)

Just for Fun *(5 minutes)*

The Beatles wrote a song called "All You Need Is Love." Do you think that holds true in marriage? Why or why not?

Video Notes *(10–15 minutes)*

Time to Discuss *(25 minutes)*

1. If your marriage could be mapped out like the cross-section of a tree, which "rings" would stand out as having a powerful effect on your relationship together?

2. A famous writer once said, "We have been poisoned by fairy tales." What fairy tale or fantasy image did you bring to your marriage early on that caused tension or misunderstanding in your relationship?

3. What do you think of the idea that a marriage can be strengthened, not *in spite of* the problems a couple faces, but *because of* them?

4. As you begin this study, what hopes and fears do you carry with you?

Time to Explore Your Workbook Exercises *(10 minutes)*

Within your small group, take time to complete Exercise 4 in your workbook. This exercise asks you to explore unmet expectations in your relationship. Every couple has them, but not every couple is aware of them. This brief exercise will raise your level of awareness in this area. Once you've done the exercise, share what you feel comfortable with. What did you learn about yourself from doing this exercise that you can share with the rest of the group? Do you identify with other people's insights from the same exercise?

Taking Time As a Couple

Spend some time this week as a couple completing Exercise 5, "The Big Question," in this workbook. It is actually a new habit you can begin to practice on a regular basis, and it is sure to raise the level of comfort and satisfaction in your relationship.

If you'd like to carve out a path together in this series, we also recommend that you do Exercise 1. It will ask you to take inventory of your relationship—something that will enable you to set your course for the weeks to come much more effectively.

tackle this problem first . . . and all others get easier

A fine line separates an obstacle from an opportunity
and it's discovered the instant a couple sees it with new eyes.
(Based on chapter 3)

Just for Fun *(5 minutes)*

Before the timer on your DVD screen runs out, list *all* the things you can see in the room around you that are green!

_____	_____	_____
_____	_____	_____
_____	_____	_____

Video Notes *(10–15 minutes)*

Time to Discuss *(25 minutes)*

1. As you survey the landscape of your marriage, what kinds of attitudes do you see? If you are like most couples, you could probably use an attitude tune-up. If so, what specific attitudes do you need to change the most?

2. Do you ever put your partner in a box by using words like "always" and "never"? As in, "You always leave your clothes on the floor," or "You're never on time"? How does this affect your spouse? Could you make a conscious effort to eliminate these words from your vocabulary—and your mind-set?

3. What do you think of the idea that everything hinges on attitude? And that, like a Hoberman Sphere, a marriage will either expand or contract based on each partner's attitudes?

4. A negative attitude can be helped by opening up a window of grace in your marriage. Describe a time when your spouse gave you the gift of grace, perhaps by withholding a complaint or an accusation at a time when you expected one? What effect did this have on you?

Time to Explore Your Workbook Exercises *(10 minutes)*

Within your small group, take the time to complete Exercise 7 in your workbook. This will help you identify your "Attitude Quotient." Share what you learned about your self-talk as a result of this exercise. Discuss how your self-talk impacts your marriage.

Taking Time As a Couple

If you would like to take your understanding of how your attitudes impact your relationship in specific terms, complete Exercise 8. It will delve into your "mind-set" and it just may be one of the most important things you do as a couple this week.

the subtle saboteurs of every marriage

Learn to defend your marriage against these sneak attacks
and you will have built an impenetrable fortress of love.
(Based on chapter 5)

Just for Fun *(5 minutes)*

Describe a time when you surprised your spouse. Was it romantic? Comical? Or maybe not so pleasant?

Video Notes *(10–15 minutes)*

Time to Discuss *(25 minutes)*

1. How has busyness crept into your marriage? Be specific. Are you feeling like your schedules have collided with romance and other things you enjoy about being a couple? What is something specific you can do this week to keep busyness from interfering with your ability to connect with your spouse?

2. Irritation or crabbiness is something few of us like to own up to, but try to identify specific times when it is most apparent. When are the times that your spouse has to "handle you with care"? How could you cope with these moments in your marriage to minimize the irritation? The more specific you can be, the better.

3. If you feel comfortable, talk about a time when you struggled with financial debt—either before marriage or as a couple. If it's an issue you faced in the past, how did you overcome it? If it's something you're dealing with now, what is one concrete thing you can do immediately to address it?

4. Of the three marital saboteurs that are discussed in the video—busyness, irritation, and debt—which one would you identify as your most damaging? What have you tried in the past to combat it and what can you do today that will make it better?

Time to Explore Your Workbook Exercises *(10 minutes)*

Busyness is a subtle saboteur for nearly every married couple—whether you have kids or not. So take the time in your group session to complete Exercise 12, "Taking Control of Your Time-Starved Marriage." Share what you learned from this exercise with the group. And pay careful attention to what others learned as well. You'll find you have much to teach each other on reclaiming your couple time together.

Taking Time As a Couple

We highly recommend that you do Exercise 13 sometime in the next week. This workbook exercise will serve as a point of connection for the two of you and help set the wheels in motion for a meaningful getaway.

how to solve any problem in five (not-so-easy) steps

Discover the "slumbering powers" in your marriage
and use this proven plan for revolutionizing your love life.
(Based on chapter 6)

Just for Fun *(5 minutes)*

It's time for a COFHE break. There are five tools every marriage can use to tackle problems, represented by the letters C, O, F, H, and E. What do you think these letters might stand for?

C _____

O _____

F _____

H _____

E _____

Video Notes *(10–15 minutes)*

Time to Discuss *(25 minutes)*

1. Do you agree that tough times can only be overcome by a couple when they each take responsibility for their own attitudes and actions? Can you recall a specific time when you did this in your marriage? What was the result?

2. Forgiveness is truly a radical method of restoration. Looking back over your married life, can you identify times when forgiveness that you either gave or received changed the course of your relationship? How so?

3. Some experts have said that hope is not as ethereal as some people have made it out to be. It is about having concrete goals. What do you think? Have you found it productive to formalize your hopes for your marriage into goals? What are some examples?

4. How often would you say you consciously put yourself in your partner's shoes? Can you think of a time when empathy changed your perspective on something in your marriage?

Time to Explore Your Workbook Exercises *(10 minutes)*

Take the time in your group to complete Exercise 17. This exercise will show you how well you are empathizing with each other. This valuable skill can always be improved and this experience will help identify any necessary improvements you can make. As always, learn from others in the group to pick up pointers on how you can apply this skill more often to your own relationship.

Taking Time As a Couple

If you'd like to drill down a bit on the idea of taking more responsibility in your relationships—a cornerstone of a healthy marriage—take the time this week to complete Exercise 15, "Owning Up." It won't take you much time, but it will pay off big dividends.

joining your spirits like never before

Deep down in the soul of your marriage is a thirst
for connection that can only be quenched when you drink
from the ultimate source of love.
(Based on chapter 7)

Just for Fun *(5 minutes)*

On a scale of 1 to 10, where would you rate your *desire* for making a spiritual connection with your spouse?

1	2	3	4	5	6	7	8	9	10

Also on a scale of 1 to 10, rate *how satisfied you are* with the current state of spiritual intimacy in your marriage?

1	2	3	4	5	6	7	8	9	10

Video Notes *(10–15 minutes)*

Time to Discuss *(25 minutes)*

1. Making and maintaining a genuine spiritual connection—the kind where a husband and wife share their spiritual sides in a reciprocal fashion and have a sense of union because of it—is often difficult for even the most devout couples. Why, in your opinion, is this the case?

2. If there is a gap between how you rated your desire for spiritual intimacy compared to how satisfied you are with spiritual intimacy in your marriage, what can you do to bring these numbers closer together?

3. Have you ever thought that your spiritual style would also be good for your partner because it works so well for you? If so, what kinds of subtle or not-so-subtle messages have you sent your partner because of this, and what might you do to rebuild any potential damage because of them?

4. Explore the issue of inspiration. What are some of the most inspirational moments you have shared as a couple? Are they easy or difficult to remember? And what might this tell you about your need for inspiration now? More important, what can you do to cultivate more inspirational moments in your marriage? Be specific.

Time to Explore Your Workbook Exercises *(10 minutes)*

Take time in your small group session to complete Exercise 18, "Assessing Your Spiritual Language." There's no guilt involved here. This is simply a tool to help you each understand how you relate to God—because, if you are like most couples, you probably don't do this in the same way. Discuss with the group how you seem to relate to God best. We think you'll enjoy hearing how others in your group follow a different pathway to God.

Taking Time As a Couple

How would you like to be inspired this week? Well, Exercise 19 can help make that happen. Take the time as a couple some-time this week to complete this exercise and your marriage will be better than you imagined it could be.

the good that comes
from a problem-solving marriage

*Every day your love expands when you clearly see you've
become a better person for having married your partner.*
(Based on chapter 8)

Just for Fun *(5 minutes)*

When you start a new job, one of the first things you learn
about is your "benefits package." If you had been handed a "marital benefits package" on your wedding day, what do you think it
would have contained?

Video Notes *(10–15 minutes)*

Time to Discuss *(25 minutes)*

1. Frederick Buechner says, "A marriage made in heaven is one where a man and a woman become more richly themselves together than the chances are either of them could ever have managed to become alone." How have you become more "richly yourself" because of your marriage?

2. Research has plainly shown that marriage can make people happier, healthier, and wealthier. The good that comes from a problem-solving marriage, of course, provides a unique blessing for each couple. Out of these three categories, which blessing do you most appreciate and why?

3. Some people find it extremely powerful to keep a record of things they are thankful for. Do you think that such an exercise, if applied to your marriage, would raise your level of appreciation for your marriage? No doubt. You might consider doing just that, but for right now, what are the two or three things you appreciate most about your marriage relationship?

Time to Explore Your Workbook Exercises *(10 minutes)*

Rather than completing a workbook exercise in this final session, we suggest you simply take a moment alone with your spouse to answer two questions. First, how has married life made you a happier person? Be specific. Second, how will your marriage be better for having gone through this six-week series? Again, be specific and feel free to review the previous five sessions as a couple to choose your answer together. When you're done discussing these questions with your spouse, take a moment to share your answers with the group.

Taking Time As a Couple

If you completed Exercise 5, "The Big Question," in the first week together as a couple, take some time this week to go back and do it again (it's never the same twice!). And even if you didn't do it at the start, try it this week. It won't take long at all and it's a terrific capstone to these six sessions.

resources by Les and Leslie Parrott

Books
Becoming Soul Mates
Getting Ready for the Wedding
I Love You More
I Love You More Workbooks
Love Is
The Love List
Love Talk
Love Talk Workbooks
The Marriage Mentor Manual
Meditations on Proverbs for Couples
Questions Couples Ask
Relationships
Relationships Workbook
Saving Your Marriage Before It Starts
Saving Your Marriage Before It Starts Workbooks
Saving Your Second Marriage Before It Starts
Saving Your Second Marriage Before It Starts Workbooks

Video Curriculum—Zondervan*Groupware*™
I Love You More
Love Talk
Mentoring Engaged and Newlywed Couples
Relationships
Saving Your Marriage Before It Starts

Audio Pages®
Love Talk
Relationships
Saving Your Marriage Before It Starts
Saving Your Second Marriage Before It Starts

Books by Les Parrott III
The Control Freak
Helping Your Struggling Teenager
High Maintenance Relationships
The Life You Want Your Kids to Live
Seven Secrets of a Healthy Dating Relationship
Shoulda, Coulda, Woulda
Once Upon a Family

Books by Leslie Parrott
If You Ever Needed Friends, It's Now
God Loves You Nose to Toes
Marshmallow Clouds

Saving Your Marriage Before It Starts

Seven Questions to Ask Before (and After) You Marry

Drs. Les and Leslie Parrott

Do you want to build a marriage that will last a lifetime? *Saving Your Marriage Before It Starts* is the first comprehensive marriage preparation program specifically designed for today's couples. And it's the first program for couples developed by a couple. And Les and Leslie Parrott are no ordinary couple. As marriage counselors and teachers, they're on the cutting edge of marriage research and education. Each year they teach a blockbuster relationships course to hundreds of college students. They see the struggles and dreams of couples up close. And they reveal the flaws and foibles of their own relationship in order to show how challenging—and rewarding—marriage can be. Most importantly, however, Les and Leslie Parrott share a dream: to equip couples in their twenties and thirties to prepare for lifelong marriage before it even starts. Les and Leslie will lead you through the thorniest spot in establishing a relationship. You'll learn how to uncover and deal with problems before they emerge. You'll discover how to communicate, not just talk. And you'll learn the importance of becoming "soul mates"—a couple committed to growing together spiritually. *Saving Your Marriage Before It Starts* is more than a book—it's practically a premarital counseling session! Questions at the end of every chapter help you explore each topic personally. Companion men's and women's workbooks full of self-tests and exercises will help you apply what you learn.

Hardcover: 0-310-49240-8

Curriculum: 0-310-20451-8

Workbook for Men: 0-310-48731-5

Workbook for Women: 0-310-48748-2

Pick up a copy today at your favorite bookstore!

ZONDERVAN™

GRAND RAPIDS, MICHIGAN 49530 USA

WWW.ZONDERVAN.COM

Love Talk
Speak Each Other's Language Like You Never Have Before

Drs. Les and Leslie Parrott

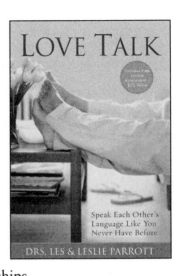

Over and over couples consistently name "improved communication" as the greatest need in their relationships. *Love Talk* —by acclaimed relationship experts Drs. Les and Leslie Parrott—is a deep yet simple plan full of new insights that will revolutionize communication in love relationships.

    Love Talk includes The Love Talk Indicator, a free personalized online assessment (a $30.00 value) to help you determine your unique talk style

Hardcover: 0-310-24596-6

Curriculum: 0-310-26467-7

Abridged Audio CD: 0-310-26214-3

Love Talk Workbooks Available

Want to get the most out of this book? The two softcover "his and hers" workbooks are full of lively exercises and enlightening self-tests that

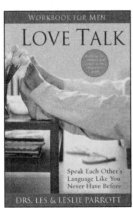

help couples apply what they are learning about communication directly to their relationships.

    Love Talk is also available as an abridged Audio Pages® CD.

Workbook for Men: 0-310-26212-7

Workbook for Women: 0-310-26213-5

Love Talk Starters
275 Questions to Get Your Conversations Going

Drs. Les and Leslie Parrott

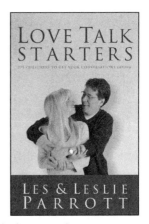

Acclaimed relationship experts Les and Leslie Parrott are back with a wonderful and insightful guide for improving the single most important factor in any marriage or love relationship—communication. In *Love Talk*, the Parrotts will help you discover you and your partner's communication style, and learn the best ways for your styles to interact. In this companion book, *Love Talk Starters*, you will find engaging, intriguing, and revealing conversation starters. Some questions are just for fun, some will educate you about your spouse's life, and still others will drill down on some more serious topics. Use these simple conversation starters and begin communicating your way into a happier, healthier, and stronger relationship today.

Softcover: 0-310-81047-7

Just the Two of Us
Love Talk Meditations for Couples

Drs. Les and Leslie Parrott

Les and Leslie Parrott share communication insights and wisdom for couples that are newly married or have been married for forty years. The Parrotts write in a very compelling and transparent way using their personal experiences with communication challenges in their own marriage. A wonderful companion to *Love Talk*. Some of the titles of the meditations include: What Were You Thinking?, You're Reading My Mind, and The Talks That Tie Us Together.

Gift book: 0-310-80381-0

The Love List

Eight Little Things That Make a Big Difference in Your Marriage

Drs. Les and Leslie Parrott

This little book will make a big impact on your marriage. Start right away applying its hands-on concepts. You'll immediately increase intimacy, gain new direction, enjoy more laughter, and much more.

You'll love how *The Love List* unites purposefulness and spontaneity. "A few small actions—practiced on a daily, weekly, monthly, and yearly basis—can change everything for a couple," say relationship experts Les and Leslie Parrott. "Little, deliberate behaviors quietly lavish love on a marriage."

Drawing on their professional insights into successful couples and sharing candidly from their own marriage, the Parrotts give you eight simple-but-powerful, instantly usable principles that will lift your marriage out of the doldrums into everything you've wanted it to be. Plus, it's also fun! Especially when you start seeing noticeable results right away.

Hardcover: 0-310-24850-7

Pick up a copy today at your favorite bookstore!

ZONDERVAN™

GRAND RAPIDS, MICHIGAN 49530 USA

WWW.ZONDERVAN.COM

Are you interested in being a marriage mentor?

Learn more about this powerful way of strengthening marriages couple to couple. Go to:

www.RealRelationships.com

Bring the Parrotts to your community!

Visit *www.RealRelationships.com*

Drs. Les and Leslie Parrott are internationally known, bestselling authors. They have been featured on *Oprah*, CBS *This Morning*, CNN, *The View*, and in *USA Today* and the *New York Times*. They are also frequent guest speakers and have written for a variety of magazines. The Parrotts are hosts of the national radio broadcast *Love Talk*.

We want to hear from you. Please send your comments about this book to us in care of zreview@zondervan.com. Thank you.

GRAND RAPIDS, MICHIGAN 49530 USA

WWW.ZONDERVAN.COM